A Four-tongued
ALPHABET

Ruth Brown

An alphabet book in four languages

Andersen Press · London

A Note on the Spanish Alphabet

The Spanish alphabet contains two additional letters which have not been illustrated in this book. The 13th letter is *ll* as in *llave* which means *key*, and the 16th letter is *ñ* as in *piña* which means *pineapple*.

A

a

ark · arche · Arche · arca

B b

ball · balle · Ball · balón

C c

chameleon · caméléon · Chamäleon · camaleón

D   d

dragon · dragon · Drache · dragón

E
e

elephant · éléphant · Elefant · elefante

F f

fire · feu · Feuer · fuego

G g

gorilla · gorille · Gorilla · gorila

H   h

hamster · hamster · Hamster · hamster

I i

insect · insecte · Insekt · insecto

J

j

jaguar · jaguar · Jaguar · jaguar

K   k

kiwi · kiwi · Kiwi · kiwi

L   l

labyrinth · labyrinthe · Labyrinth · laberinto

M m

magic · magie · Magie · magia

N   n

nose · nez · Nase · nariz

O   o

orchid · orchidée · Orchidee · orquidea

P p

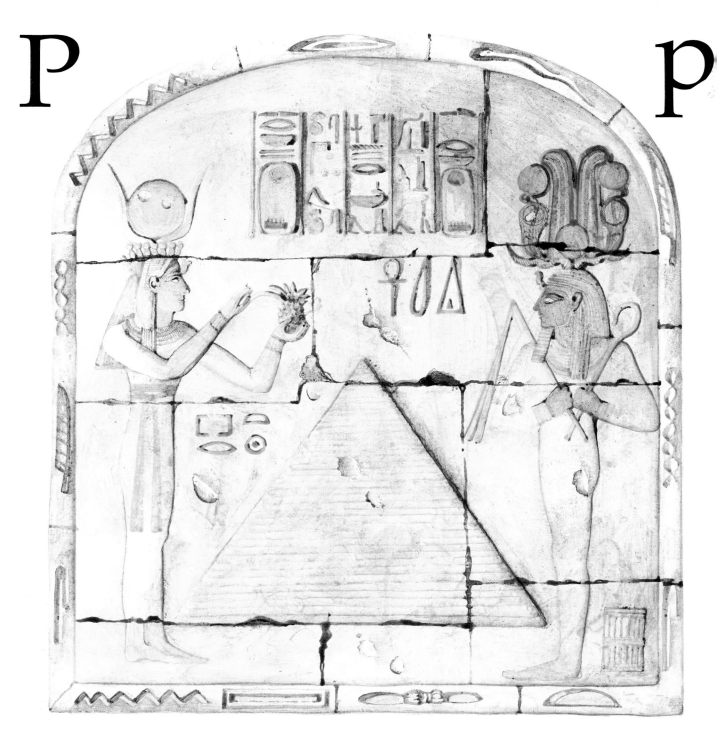

pyramid · pyramide · Pyramide · pirámide

quintet · quintette · Quintett · quinteto

R r

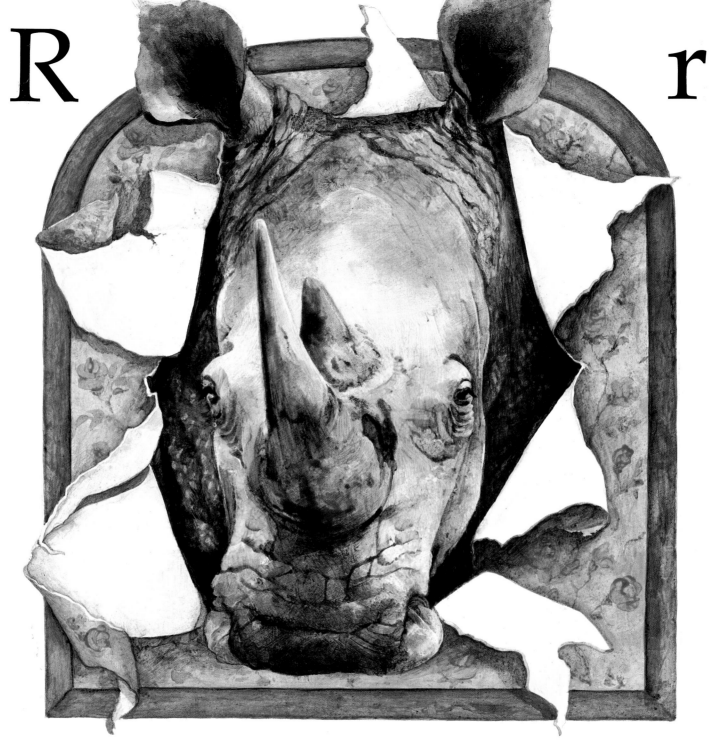

rhinoceros · rhinocéros · Rhinozeros · rinoceronte

S   S

snake · serpent · Schlange · serpiente

T t

tiger · tigre · Tiger · tigre

U u

universe · univers · Universum · universo

V   V

volcano · volcan · Vulkan · volcán

W w

water-polo · water-polo · Wasserball · water-polo

X   x

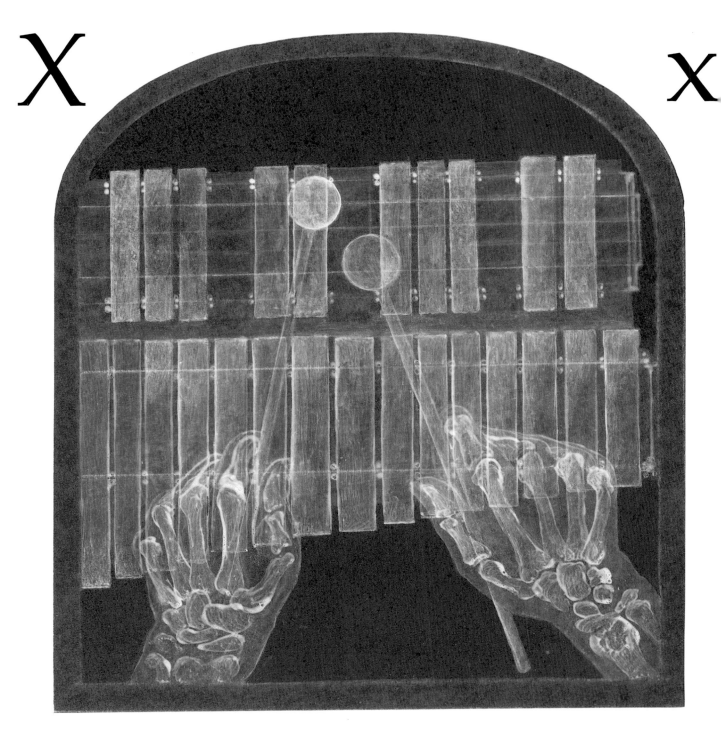

xylophone · xylophone · Xylophon · xilófono

Y y

yeti · yeti · Yeti · yeti

Z
Z

zigzag · zigzag · Zickzack · zigzag

		English	**French**	**German**	**Spanish**
A	a	ark	arche	Arche	arca
B	b	ball	balle	Ball	balón
C	c	chameleon	caméléon	Chamäleon	camaleón
D	d	dragon	dragon	Drache	dragón
E	e	elephant	éléphant	Elefant	elefante
F	f	fire	feu	Feuer	fuego
G	g	gorilla	gorille	Gorilla	gorila
H	h	hamster	hamster	Hamster	hamster
I	i	insect	insecte	Insekt	insecto
J	j	jaguar	jaguar	Jaguar	jaguar
K	k	kiwi	kiwi	Kiwi	kiwi
L	l	labyrinth	labyrinthe	Labyrinth	laberinto
M	m	magic	magie	Magie	magia
N	n	nose	nez	Nase	nariz
O	o	orchid	orchidée	Orchidee	orquidea
P	p	pyramid	pyramide	Pyramide	pirámide
Q	q	quintet	quintette	Quintett	quinteto
R	r	rhinoceros	rhinocéros	Rhinozeros	rinoceronte
S	s	snake	serpent	Schlange	serpiente
T	t	tiger	tigre	Tiger	tigre
U	u	universe	univers	Universum	universo
V	v	volcano	volcan	Vulkan	volcán
W	w	water-polo	water-polo	Wasserball	water-polo
X	x	xylophone	xylophone	Xylophon	xilófono
Y	y	yeti	yeti	Yeti	yeti
Z	z	zigzag	zigzag	Zickzack	zigzag